The Book of Daniel

*The Secret Story of Princes and Pirates,
Rogues, Revolutionaries, and Freemasons
In North and South Carolina*

By

Stephen Payseur

The Book of Daniel

*The Secret Story of Princes and Pirates,
Rogues, Revolutionaries, and Freemasons
In North and South Carolina*

By

Stephen Payseur

Copyright 2012, All Rights Reserved

Library of Congress Number 2012908256

ISBN **978-0-9656697-4-0**

Cover Design by Shannon Vernitsky

Table of Contents

Author's Preface

Chapter 1	How It All Began	7
Chapter 2	The Palatine and Immigration to America	11
Chapter 3	The Lost Dauphin	19
Chapter 4	Peter Stuart Ney	37
Chapter 5	Jean Laffite	47
Chapter 6	Marquis de Lafayette	55
Chapter 7	Daniel Payseur	63
Chapter 8	Jonas Payseur	69
Chapter 9	Jesse James	75
Chapter 10	Lewis Cass Payseur	81
Chapter 11	Epilog	93

References   99

Illustrations

Louis XVI	21
Marie Antoinette	25
Louis Charles, The Lost Dauphin	33
Daniel Payseur Tombstone	35, 36
Michel Ney	39
Jean Laffite	53
Marquis de Lafayette	57
Jonas Payseur	71
Jesse James	77
Lewis Cass Payseur	83

Author's Preface

What you are about to read is, what I think, a very interesting story. It is a story of lies and deception. More importantly, it is a story of a small corner of North Carolina and primarily one of the families who lives there. It is a story of connections.

Many people have asked me if this tale is true. I can honestly say that I have no idea. I am certain that much of what you read here is not true. Some of what you will read here is definitely true. The task for the reader is to determine for him or herself what to believe.

One thing needs to be kept in mind as you read this book. Over the years, the name, Payseur, has been spelled many ways. Pasour, Paysour, Paseur, Payseur, Besour, Beseur, are just a few of them. My grandfather spelled his name, Payseur, yet some of his brothers and sisters spelled theirs, Paysour. Many of these spellings I will use interchangeably throughout.

After much research, I decided to put everything down in this narrative for the reader to decide. There are way too many coincidences for all of this to be false and way too many assumptions for all of it to be true. However, here it is. I hope you enjoy. I hope it makes you think, and I hope it makes you want to look further into other so-called "facts."

Steve Payseur, 2012

Chapter 1

How it All Began

About fifteen years ago, I was poking around on the internet. I was looking for nothing in particular, just letting one thing lead me to another. I call these "non searches." Often when I had done similar non-searches I ran across very interesting topics. Many of these were funny, or informative, or even just weird.

Sometimes I would share these with friends and family, usually the funny ones. Others were a little more compelling, like the one about the Lincoln County Witch. That one was disturbing inasmuch as I had known many of the people involved in that sordid tale. Maybe that will be another book, but it would be much better if the family involved wrote that story. After all, they lived it and know the facts better than any researcher could ever know.

On this particular day, I decided to search the web to see what, if anything, was on there about me. Surprisingly I found several dozen references to me. Most of them were obscure references to things I had done at some point and would never be very interesting to anyone. Most weren't even very interesting to me and I was the subject of those references. I decided to broaden my search to include only my family name, Payseur.

I must digress a bit here. A few years before I began my research I bought a book by Thomas Marino. Marino was a linear descendant of the original Payseur who had arrived in America 200 years ago. He had painstakingly compiled the genealogy of the Payseur clan after many years of research. My father, Bob Payseur and my cousin, Greg Payseur had supplied Mr. Marino with much of the information he had collected about my branch of the family.

Since I had Thomas Marino's book, **Pasour, Paysour, Payseur, Together Again**,[i] I had begun my own genealogical research. I wasn't looking for just names and dates, I wanted to find stories about these individuals if I could. It was a whole lot easier to look than it was to find, as I discovered very quickly.

My father and my cousin, Greg, were doing the same thing. My father put together a family tree and began to catalog births, deaths and marriages in our more immediate extended family.

Greg began to branch out a little more than that. He was following the branches of the family and doing quite a bit of tracing back the ancestry of related families. Greg had found connections to many famous people from history, such as Daniel Boone. These were quite interesting to most of us. Greg began to send me updates of the more interesting things that he had found.

He has never stopped doing that. He probably has hundreds of thousands of names in his database by now.

Early on, one of the more interesting things that I found was our family connection to Macbeth, the Scottish King of Shakespeare's play. That connection was through the Beattie family. This connection would turn up again later.

There were very many spellings of our name. Some brothers and sisters even spelled their names differently. They were scattered all over the country, though most were found in several locations such as North Carolina, Pennsylvania, Ohio, and Alabama.

Most histories and genealogies stated that our family came from Germany, though some said France. I had trouble trying to resolve this contradiction.

Continuing my research, I started to find some incredible information, which I referred to my father and to Greg. Both found these new pieces of information to be very interesting. Greg in particular began trying some face to face interviewing, and becoming an amateur private eye.

We have found connections with the Pirate Jean Lafitte, Napoleon's Marshal Michel Ney, Abraham Lincoln, A.A. Springs, Jesse James, Louis XVI, King George III, the Knights Templar, the Illuminati, and many more. I, and no one else, have been able to confirm most of these connections. However, the more we look into them, the more questions and coincidences seem to pop up. In other words, the more I know, the more I don't know.

The following pages will put forth the efforts of my research in pretty much straightforward manner. Many people will think it is all a work of fiction. Maybe it is. Then again, I believe that there is more to the story than many would think. I prefer to call it "speculative nonfiction." You be the judge.

Chapter 2

The Palatine and Immigration to America

The country of Germany as we know it has really not been a unified country for very long. For much of its history it has been a loose association of small provinces or even city-states each ruled by its own ruler. In fact, in the year 1792, there were coincidentally 1792 of these states in Germany. Obviously, since then there has been much consolidation until now Germany is a prosperous unified state.

One of the regions of Germany is called the Palatine. The Palatine area lies on the western border and joins the borders of France and Switzerland. The Alsace and Lorraine regions of France are contiguous with the Palatine.

For those familiar with the history of this area, you know that the Alsace / Lorraine area has been in contention for many, many years. Wars have been fought there as long as anyone can remember, and both Alsace and Lorraine have changed back and forth from being German Provinces to French Provinces. This depended on who the winner of the last war was. This movement from French to German, German to French will prove to have some significance in this story.

Because of this back and forth conquest, many people of the Palatine were French speakers and many people in the Alsace / Lorraine region were German speakers.

The following is a brief history of the Palatine area..

PALATINE HISTORY

by Lorine McGinnis Schulze
Olive Tree Genealogy http://olivetreegenealogy.com/
Copyright © 1996

    The Palatinate or German PFALZ, was, in German history, the land of the Count Palatine, a title held by a leading secular prince of the Holy Roman Empire. Geographically, the Palatinate was divided between two small territorial clusters: the Rhenish, or Lower Palatinate, and the Upper Palatinate. The Rhenish Palatinate included lands on both sides of the Middle Rhine River between its Main and Neckar tributaries. Its capital until the 18th century was Heidelberg. The Upper Palatinate was located in northern Bavaria, on both sides of the Naab River as it flows south toward the Danube and extended eastward to the Bohemian Forest. The boundaries of the Palatinate varied with the political and dynastic fortunes of the Counts Palatine.

    The Palatinate has a border beginning in the north, on the Moselle River about 35 miles southwest of Coblenz to Bingen and east to Mainz, down the Rhine River to Oppenheim, Guntersblum and Worms, then continuing eastward above the Nieckar River about 25 miles east of Heidelberg then looping back westerly below Heidelberg to Speyer, south down the Rhine River to Alsace, then north-westerly back up to its beginning on the Moselle River.

    The first Count Palatine of the Rhine was Hermann I, who received the office in 945. Although not originally hereditary, the title was held mainly by his descendants until his line expired in 1155, and the Bavarian Wittelsbachs took over in 1180. In 1356, the Golden Bull (a papal bull: an official document, usually commands from the Pope and sealed with the official Papal seal called a Bulla) made the Count Palatine an Elector of the Holy Roman Empire.

During the Reformation, the Palatinate accepted Protestantism and became the foremost Calvinist region in Germany.

After Martin Luther published his 95 Theses on the door of the castle church at Wittenberg on 31 October 1517, many of his followers came under considerable religious persecution for their beliefs. Perhaps for reasons of mutual comfort and support, they gathered in what is known as the Palatine. These folk came from many places, Germany, Holland, Switzerland and beyond, but all shared a common view on religion.

The protestant Elector Palatine Frederick V (1596-1632), called the "Winter King" of Bohemia, played a unique role in the struggle between Roman Catholic and Protestant Europe. His election in 1619 as King of Bohemia precipitated the Thirty Years War that lasted from 1619 until 1648. Frederick was driven from Bohemia and in 1623, deposed as Elector Palatine.

During the Thirty Years War, the Palatine country and other parts of Germany suffered from the horrors of fire and sword as well as from pillage and plunder by the French armies. This war was based upon both politics and religious hatreds, as the Roman Catholic armies sought to crush the religious freedom of a politically-divided Protestantism.

Many unpaid armies and bands of mercenaries, both of friends and foe, devoured the substance of the people and by 1633, even the catholic French supported the Elector Palatine for a time for political reasons.

During the War of the Grand Alliance (1689-97), the troops of the French monarch Louis XIV ravaged the Rhenish Palatinate, causing many Germans to emigrate. Many of the early German settlers of America (e.g. the Pennsylvania Dutch) were refugees from the Palatinate. During the French Revolutionary and Napoleonic Wars, the Palatinate's lands on the west bank of the

Rhine were incorporated into France, while its eastern lands were divided largely between neighbouring Baden and Hesse.

Nearly the entire 17th century in central Europe was a period of turmoil as Louis XIV of France sought to increase his empire. The War of the Palatinate (as it was called in Germany), aka The War of The League of Augsburg, began in 1688 when Louis claimed the Palatinate. Every large city on the Rhine above Cologne was sacked. The War ended in 1697 with the Treaty of Ryswick. The Palatinate was badly battered but still outside French control. In 1702, the War of the Spanish Succession began in Europe and lasted until 1713, causing a great deal of instability for the Palatines. The Palatinate lay on the western edge of the Holy Roman Empire not far from France's eastern boundary. Louis wanted to push his eastern border to the Rhine, the heart of the Palatinate.

While the land of the Palatinate was good for its inhabitants, many of whom were farmers, vineyard operators etc., its location was unfortunately subject to invasion by the armies of Britain, France, and Germany. Mother Nature also played a role in what happened, for the winter of 1708 was particularly severe and many of the vineyards perished. So, as well as the devastating effects of war, the Palatines were subjected to the winter of 1708-09, the harshest in 100 years.

The scene was set for a mass migration. At the invitation of Queen Anne in the spring of 1709, about 7 000 harassed Palatines sailed down the Rhine to Rotterdam. From there, about 3000 were dispatched to America, either directly or via England, under the auspices of William Penn. The remaining 4 000 were sent via England to Ireland to strengthen the protestant interest.

Although the Palatines were scattered as agricultural settlers over much of Ireland, major accumulations were found in Counties Limerick and Tipperary. As the years progressed and dissatisfactions increased, many of these folk seized opportunities to join their compatriots in Pennsylvania, or to go to newly-opened settlements in Canada.

There were many reasons for the desire of the Palatines to emigrate to the New World: oppressive taxation, religious bickering, hunger for more and better land, the advertising of the English colonies in America and the favourable attitude of the British government toward settlement in the North American colonies. Many of the Palatines believed they were going to Pennsylvania, Carolina or one of the tropical islands.

The passage down the Rhine took from 4 to 6 weeks. Tolls and fees were demanded by authorities of the territories through which they passed. Early in June, the number of Palatines entering Rotterdam reached 1 000 per week. Later that year, the British government issued a Royal proclamation in German that all arriving after October 1709 would be sent back to Germany. The British could not effectively handle the number of Palatines in London and there may have been as many as 32 000 by November 1709. They wintered over in England since there were no adequate arrangements for the transfer of the Palatines to the English colonies.

In 1710, three large groups of Palatines sailed from London. The first went to Ireland, the second to Carolina and the third to New York with the new Governor, Robert Hunter. There were 3 000 Palatines on 10 ships that sailed for NY and approximately 470 died on the voyage or shortly after their arrival.

In NY, the Palatines were expected to work for the British authorities, producing naval stores [tar and pitch] for the navy in return for their passage to NY. They were also expected to act as a buffer between the French and Natives on the northern frontier and the English colonies to the south and east.

After the defeat of Napoleon (1814-15), the Congress of Vienna gave the east-bank lands of the Rhine valley to Bavaria. These lands, together with some surrounding territories, again took the name of Palatinate in 1838. **Permission to reprint** *is granted provided the following terms are followed: This article may be reproduced as long as it is not changed in any way, all identifyingURLs and copyright information remain intact (including* *this permission), and a link is provided back to Olive Tree Genealogy http://olivetreegenealogy.com/ 0[ii]*

It was in this area and this time that the Payseur family is first noted. As with many families, the spelling has changed over the years. Most notably is the fact that the German "B" and the German "P" sound very similar, so these letters are often interchanged. Names were often spelled phonetically by registrars and tax collectors as many people of the time could neither read or write.

The first record that we have of the Payseur family dates back to Hans Jacob Boshaar. He was born in 1647 to Hans Albrecht and Anna Margaret Boshaar in Zweibrucken, Germany.[iii] It should be noted that historian I.D. Rupp, a descendant of the Bashores, claimed that the name was actually French Huguenot. According to Rupp the Le Baiseurs moved to the Palatine sometime after 1614 due to religious persecution in France. After living in Germany for some time, the name was corrupted in both spelling and pronunciation to Bashore.

As you may recall, it was mentioned earlier that the Palatine bordered the French Provinces of Alsace and Lorraine and that many residents migrated back and forth between the German and French side. This will have some significance in later chapters.

The best that we can determine, John George Bashore was the first of the family to live in North Carolina. He was born in Lebanon County, PA in 1720 and lived to the ripe old age of 98. George was buried in the old Bethel Church Cemetery in what is now Gaston County in 1818. The spelling of John George Bashore's name changed many times after he left Pennsylvania. At various times it was Bayzour, Besour and finally Pasour. After the birth of his children, he was known in North Carolina as George Pasour, Sr.

George Pasour, Sr. and his wife, Charlotta Hetzer Pasour, had 7 children. The only one of those children with significance to this book is George Pasour, Jr.

George Pasour, Jr. was born in Maryland in 1764. George, Jr. married Hannah Hoyle, the daughter of Elizabeth Brooks Hoyl and Jacob Hoyl in 1780 in Lincoln County, NC. They had 8 children. Once again we will primarily be discussing one of them, Daniel Pasour. In November of 1851, George Jr. died and was buried in the Kastner (Costner) Cemetery in Gaston County, NC.[iv]

Now the question arises as to why the emphasis on the Payseur family. Besides the obvious interest of the author, there are a few other things that will come to light. The Payseur family members are key figures into what has sometimes been called the secret history of the Lincoln and Gaston County areas of North Carolina. As we go along, these events and persons will be discussed in greater detail.

Chapter 3

The Lost Dauphin

After the American Revolution most of the monarchies in Europe were uneasy. They were afraid that the radical concept of government by the common people would somehow take hold in Europe and elsewhere. This was a particularly worrisome feeling in both England and France.

In England, King George III was still smarting from the loss of his most valuable colonies, the American colonies. It also didn't help England's reputation as a military force, when their army and navy could not suppress that revolution. At that time England was the world's major superpower

There was also concern in France. France had aided the American Colonies in their struggle against England. Of course the French knew that the English were not too happy about that aid and weren't quite certain what the English had in mind for them.

There was also concern that Frenchmen returning from the war in America would begin to think that perhaps the common Frenchman could run his native country just like the Americans were. Those were valid concerns as the French Revolution a few years later would prove.

As much as England and France were suspicious of each other, the monarchies were even more suspicious of their citizens. Monarchies all over Europe, as much as they despised the American

Revolution, were even more concerned with preserving their own monarchy. After all it was a pretty good life being the King.

As the French Revolution progressed to the ouster of the King and Queen, and then Napoleon began his conquest of Continental Europe, it seemed as if the world was turning upside down.

After the painting by P. Duménil, Gallery of Versailles, France
LOUIS XVI.

Louis XVI

Not only did the revolution succeed in France, but King Louis XVI and his wife, Marie Antoinette, the Queen were imprisoned along with their children. In 1793 the impossible occurred. Both King Louis XVI and his Queen, Marie Antoinette, were beheaded in public on the guillotine. Shockwaves radiated throughout Europe.

At their deaths King Louis XVI and Marie Antoinette had two surviving children, Marie-Therese and Louis Charles, the Dauphin. The word dauphin at the time meant the eldest son of the King of France. In other words the heir to the throne. Both of the children were imprisoned with their parents.

After her parent's execution, Marie Therese was exiled to Austria to live with her mother's family. She lived for a while in England and Russia and finally died of pneumonia in what was then Austria in 1851. She was 73 years old.

The story of Louis Charles, the Dauphin is a little more confusing and mysterious. Rumors have persisted over the years that he Dauphin did not die in prison as the official record attests. Instead many believe that he somehow escaped and lived in secret elsewhere. In 2000, Louis Charles remains were exhumed and DNA tests were conducted. It was determined that this DNA matched the DNA of Marie Antoinette's living Austrian relatives.

That did not end the controversy however. It seems that maternal DNA can only prove that the person tested is somehow related to the mother's family. It cannot be proven from just that DNA test that the person is actually a direct linear descendant. In fact, the maternal DNA only served to corroborate one of the stories circulating about the Lost Dauphin. Here is the story.

In October of 1793, Marie Antoinette climbed the steps to the scaffold and was beheaded just like her husband before her. Reportedly her last words were, "I am sorry for what I have done."

She said this because she had stepped on the foot of one of the men waiting on the scaffold. Still locked away I prison were her 2 surviving children, Marie-Therese and the young Dauphin, Louis Charles.[v]

    There were many in the country who wanted to see the young Louis Charles, now nominally Louis XVII to take his rightful throne. One of those was a man named Toulan. He was known for his loyalty to the throne. So much so that he had been given the nickname, Fidele, by the Queen. He had been working for some time to have the royal family released from prison with no success.

Marie Antoinette

He and a group of other people continued to work for the release of the young King, only 8 years old. His group included the Marquis Jarjayes and Dr. Naudin and Dr. Saunier. The money behind thee loyalists was a member of the privileged class, Prince de Conde. The plan was to somehow free Louis Charles, then to move him to Vendee, which was a staunchly loyalist area. There he could be secluded, hidden, and protected until he could assert his rightful claim to the throne.[vi]

The plan they concocted was to replace the young King with another young boy of similar size and build and then spirit Louis Charles away. The Marquis Jarjayes had found such a boy, cousin of the young King. This young boy was very sick. Dr. Naudin was sent to confirm that this boy could pass for Louis. He confirmed that the boy was suffering from a form of scrofula, which would eventually render his limbs useless. He was deaf, and the disease he suffered from and damaged his brain. He no longer was coherent on the rare occasions when he tried to speak.[vii]

There were two people who worked in the prison, a Mr. and Mrs. Simon who were persuaded to assist Marquis Jarjayes and Dr. Naudin in freeing Louis Charles. They were promised a house in the country far from the prison and 600 pieces of gold.

The young Louis Charles, himself was not well. The dampness of the cell he was kept in and the abuse he had suffered had taken a toll on his health. He had requested some toys to play with and the Public Safety Committee had consented to his request. Mr. Simon was in charge of finding the hobbyhorse that Louis Charles had requested.

While Simon was finding the hobbyhorse, Dr. Naudin was visiting the prison every day. He insisted that the young king was ill and suggested that his long luxurious hair be cut short, so that his brain would not over heat. In reality it was because his replacement had short hair. Mrs. Simon cut Louis Charles hair.

The date had been set for the switch. On that morning Dr. Naudin and Toulan picked up the hobbyhorse they had purchased from a local toy store. It had a hollow body and was quite large. Dr. Naudin drugged the replacement child and placed him inside the horse hollow body. They took the horse to the prison and left it in the cell with Louis Charles.

Later that night the switch was made. Mr. Simon went into the cell and removed the replacement boy from the horse and dressed him in the King's clothes. The King was dressed as a peasant and hidden the washwoman's, Mrs. Simon, laundry basket.[viii]

The next morning Toulan arrived to help the Simons move to their new home in the country. Among their belongings was one very large laundry basket containing Louis Charles, Louis XVII, the Boy King of France. This was on January 19, 1794.

The carriage drove slowly to the country until they came to the village of Porte Macon where a washerwoman was waiting. They unloaded the basket form their carriage and placed it in the carriage of the washerwoman. This was no ordinary washerwomen. She was actually the Marquis e Jarjayes disguised in women's clothing.. The Marquis delivered the King into the protection of Prince de Conde in Vendee.

The young King stayed in seclusion at Vendee for several years hardly ever leaving the palace. During that time he was instructed as to which of the revolutionaries were an extreme danger to his safety and which members of the French nobility could not be trusted. After a period of time, it was decided that laving Vendee would be the safest option for Louis Charles. Prince de Conde decided to put him into the care of the one person no one would ever suspect, General Kleber.

Jean-Baptiste Kleber was born in the Alsace region (that province again) in 1753. He was one of Napoleon's most successful generals. He was known for his reluctance to fight and his disdain for his superiors. However, once he was engaged in battle, he fought to win. The Napoleonic Guide states, "Kleber shone during the campaign fighting well at Alexandria, El Arish, Jaffa, Acre and in independent command at Mt Tabor, where he held off vastly superior numbers" (http://www.napoleonguide.com/kleber.htm)[ix]

Louis Charles was given a folder full of papers identifying him and confirming his true identity, which was placed with General Kleber for safekeeping. He was made Kleber's ward and attaché and aided him in the battles in Egypt, Syria and other places. All through this time he was introduced to others as Kleber's nephew, Louis.

While they were in Egypt with Napoleon, Louis became sick and it was decided that he should return to France for his health. He did so in 1799, leaving his mentor, Kleber in Egypt. Shortly after Louis's return to France, Kleber was assassinated by a knife-wielding fanatic in Cairo.

Louis was at that point living with and working as an attaché to General Desiaix. Papers were sent to Desiax after Kleber's death naming Louis as his only heir. Kleber had become a very rich man from inheritance and from the spoils of war. He left Louis the equivalent of $1 million dollars.[x]

Again it was decided that France was becoming too unsafe for Louis. So, with assistance from many people, Louis escaped across the channel to England. He stayed in England for some time and was taken under the wing by Queen Charlotte of Mecklenburg, King George III wife. The city of Charlotte, NC and the county in which it resides, Mecklenburg, were named after her.

It is likely that Queen Charlotte was a relative of Louis considering both Charlotte's and his mother, Marie Antoinette's Austrian/Germanic heritage.

It was about this time, while the 16 year old Louis was under the protection of Queen Charlotte, that Napoleon discovered his identity and whereabouts. The English royal Family, fearing for Louis's safety, decided that America was probably the safest place for him to be. This would be far from Napoleon's reach.[xi]

The weighmaster for Louis' father, Louis VXI, was also living in England at this time. He was another person from the Alsace Lorraine area and his name was George Peseur. The word peseur in French means weighmaster. In other words, he was in charge of weighing out the gold and silver to pay the employees and purchases of the Royal Court, the paymaster. During that time, many people were known by their profession and often took their professional name as their surname. For example, Carpenter, Cooper, Mason, Baker, Knight, Smith, Fisher, and many others were very common. Louis XVII assumed the identity of Daniel Peseur, the paymaster's son and they sailed to America. King George had furnished a ship and enough provisions and money to enable them to get settled in.

One very wrong or incorrect thing that is posted widely on the internet is that Daniel purchased a number of shares in the Virginia Company.

The Virginia Company was formed by King James I, by charter, in 1606 to help promote the colonization of the new American colonies. Much stock was sold and other fundraising measures were used, including lotteries, to finance the colonization efforts.

Many wild claims were used to entice people to invest. One of the more popular ones was there was large quantities of gold to be found in the New World. That didn't quite "pan out" for the investors, if you will excuse the pun.

Besides advocating and encouraging colonization, the main objective of the Virginia Company was to make money for its investors. They hoped to achieve this by having settler succeed in Virginia and the Carolinas. They would then export to England, pay taxes and tariffs and everyone would profit.

In 1622, the Charter was revoked for the Virginia Company as the result of an Indian massacre. Both Virginia and Carolina became Crown Colonies, meaning that any and all profits went directly to the Crown and the King's designees, not to stock holders. There were none anymore.

Since Daniel was not born until the late 1700s, it would have been impossible to buy shares in a company that had been out of business for over 150 years. Checking the facts on things that are posted on the internet can sometimes be very enlightening. Especially when many of the conspiracy theorists keep citing each other. The Payseur story has enough mystery and intrigue without fabricating facts that can very easily be disproven.

There had also been a promise from the Royalists in France and from King George III that there would be people in the area where Daniel was moving who would give him aid, comfort and protection as needed. More on this later when we discuss other characters in this story.

Many histories like this one state that Daniel Pesour bought shares in the Virginia Company before he left England for America. That was impossible as the Virginia Company was dissolved by King James in 1624 when he made Virginia a Royal Colony.

They decided to sail to North Carolina and landed at Bodie Island on the North Carolina Outer Banks. The Bodie family had been granted the land on and around Bodie Island, as they were relatives of King George III.

After a short stay with the Bodies, George and Daniel Peseur moved to the frontier of North Carolina near present day Dallas, NC for two reasons. The first and most important reason, was the difficulty anyone would have in tracking down the young monarch. Second, there was already a family residing in the area who were distant relatives of the Peseurs (Le Beiseur), the Bashores from the Palatine via Pennsylvania, now calling themselves, Paseur or Pasour. They could fit right in by only changing one letter in their surname.

To give George and Daniel Pesour a cover story, King George granted George 600 acres of land in North Carolina. Since this was after the Revolutionary War, this would have been impossible for a British Sovereign to be giving away land in a separate and sovereign country. The Monarchy was fully aware of that.

King George III drafted a land grand to George Pesour and back dated it to 1749. The newly independent United States of America had made a practice of honoring land grants that had been awarded prior to their independence. This one was no exception, even though it turned up many years later.[xii]

Here is a portion of that grant:

"Granted... to George Bashore of Alsace, France... by His Majesty George II, of England. Ye parcel of land measuring 600 acres in ye district of Tryon in ye Province of Carolina and Anno Domini, 1749".[xiii]

Most of the land grants in this area were not issued until the 1760s, so this one was unique. Another curious thing was that in 1749 there was no Tryon County. It was not formed until 8 years after King George II's reign in 1768 and divided into Rutherford and

Lincoln Counties in 1779. Still the deed was accepted and George's rights enforced.

George Pesour, now Paseur, died in 1851 and the land and all his possessions passed on to his "son" Daniel Paseur.

Louis Charles

The "Lost Dauphin"

Thomas Marino, in his excellent book ***Pasour, Paysour, Payseur, Paseur Together Again,*** disputes the dates for Daniel Paseur's birth. He shows that Daniel was born on September 13, 1793 in Lincoln County, NC. Of course the Dauphin of France Louis Charles birthdate is stated as March 27, 1785 in Paris. That is an 8 year difference. This is easy to explain or at least to give a plausible explanation.[xiv]

With so many forged documents and changing names to allow the Prince to escape, one f the simplest would be to show that one or the other was either too old or too young to possibly be Louis XVII. It would seem that the discrepancy would have little relevance.

This shows the connection between the Royal family of France and the Payseur Family of NC. We will pick back up with this connection as we move through this odd tale.

Daniel Paysour Tombstone

The "Lost Dauphin"

Daniel Paysour Tombstone

The "Lost Dauphin"

Chapter 4

Peter Stuart Ney

A ship, the Lagonier, pulled into Charleston, SC harbor in January of 1816. Disembarking from this ship was a tall, thin man who identified himself as Peter Stuart Ney. He didn't stay in Charleston very long. Several people there approached him and asked if he was Napoleon's top General, Marshal Michel Ney. He vigorously denied it and soon left Charleston for good.

He became a teacher and for a short time taught at Catawba Springs Academy in Lincoln County, NC near present day Denver, NC. He shortly moved to Rowan County, NC and lived the remainder of his life there.

There was no doubt that Peter S. Ney was a Frenchman. The accent was unmistakable. He also was regal in bearing and was an expert at fencing by all accounts.

So, who was Peter S. Ney and what is his significance to this story? Many people believed that he was actually Marshal Michel Ney, Napoleon's General. However, the historic documents state that Marshal Ney was executed by firing squad in France in December, 1815.

In December of 1815 Marshal Michel Ney was led to the Luxembourg Palace Garden to face the firing squad. This in itself was unusual as the normal means of execution in France at this time was the dreaded guillotine. The location of the execution was also unusual. At the last minute the location had been changed to the Palace Garden This meant that there would be very few spectators, as most had gone to the previously announced location.[xv]

Ney, wearing a dark suit, walked into the garden. He wore no restraints and was not tied or chained. He walked to the wall turned to face the firing squad. Stepped 3 paces forward. Stopped and raised his hand. The command to "Present Arms" is given and

Ney returns the salute to the men. He then walked over to the presiding officer, Major de Saint Bias and spoke briefly with him.

Major de Saint Bias gave the command, "Ready, Aim---" The command to "Fire" came from Ney himself, bringing his hand down sharply to his chest.

When the order to fire was given, shots from 12 muskets rang out only about 30 feet where Marshal Ney stood. He fell forward. Dead. Blood poured out onto the cobblestone of the courtyard.

A spectator exclaimed, "They've killed Marshal Ney!"[xvi]

Something, however, did not seem to be exactly right. Ney had fallen forward. The official report to King Louis XVIII stated that all 12 musket balls had struck Ney, killing him instantly. Being hit with 12 musket balls from 30 feet or less should have propelled him backward not forward.

Marshal Ney's body was placed on a stretcher, covered and removed from the garden. The body remained in the hospital until six o'clock the next morning when it was removed and buried in a secret location.

Another mystery was that during this entire time, during the execution and the body's repose in the hospital, his wife of 13 years never came by. By all accounts she loved Marshal Michel Ney very much, but she never saw him after his death. Questions began to arise as to whether Marshal Ney was actually executed. For two hundred years these question have bothered many historians. But maybe there is an answer to these questions.

So, why was Ney executed in the first place?

When Napoleon began his conquest of most of Europe, Ney was one of his top generals. In fact, Napoleon had once remarked that Marshal Michel Ney was "the bravest of the brave."

Michel Ney
Marshal of France

When Napoleon was defeated and exiled to the island of Elba, King Louis XVIII, though he didn't completely trust them, entreated Napoleon's former generals to support the monarchy. As Louis the VXI's brother, Louis VXIII had assumed the throne. The rightful heir, his brother's son Louis Charles was presumed dead.

As you remember, by this time the Crown Prince, Louis Charles, had secretly fled to America with the royal weigh master, George Pesour. Louis Charles had changed his name to Daniel Pesour and with assistance from England's George III had settled on a 600 acre land grant in North Carolina.

Napoleon's exile on Elba lasted only about a year when he invaded the south of France with a small army determined to once again become the Emperor. He took Grenoble without firing a shot. All the soldiers at Grenoble refused to fight and changed sides supporting Napoleon.

This turn of events worried Louis XVII, and though he didn't entirely trust Napoleon's marshals that he had inherited, had no choice but to assemble them and the army and try to stop Napoleon's advance toward Paris. When Marshal Ney was summoned to the Royal Court, he promised the King to return Napoleon to Paris in an "iron cage."[xvii]

Ney and his army were sent to engage Napoleon. When the 2 armies met, they stood in silence facing each other for a long time. The silence was finally broken when Napoleon rode to the front. At that time a cry went out from Ney's army. They shouted "Vive l 'Emperor, " broke ranks, and joined Napoleon's army. Ney rode forward and greeted his former emperor. Napoleon asked Ney to join his cause and Ney agreed.

This entire force began their advance toward Paris. Upon hearing what had happened, King Louis XVIII fled to the safety of Belgium. Napoleon was back in charge. It stayed this way until Napoleon suffered his final defeat by Wellington at Waterloo less than 100 days later.

The following is taken from an article by Thomas Gregory, **Peter Stuart Ney, Freemason, Marshal of Napoleon**
http://blackmerlodge.org/wp-content/uploads/2010/12/PETER-STUART-NEY.pdf

With the King back in power, a list of traitors was drawn up. Near the top of that list was the name of Marshal Michel Ney. The Chamber of Peers found Ney guilty of treason and ordered his execution by firing squad. At his trial Ney spoke, "Yes, I am French – I will die French!"

In his book, **Marshal Ney : a Dual Life,** *Legette Blythe states that Wellington had intervened, his being a Freemason, a member of a lodge in County Meath in Ireland.[xviii] Dr. Edward J. Smoot, author of* **Marshal Ney, Before and After Execution***, states, "I believe that Wellington saved Ney's life, and in all probability, did not wish to intervene publicly. A mock execution would serve his purposes, everything considered, and Ney at the same time, would be sufficiently punished."*

King Louis decided to send the man he trusted most, Charles Talleyrand-Perigord, to Vienna for the peace conference, while at home the arrests and trials began in earnest.

Talleyrand served as an ambassador and as Minister of Foreign Affairs. He helped form the provisional government but by late 1815 was forced to resign due to the hostility of the Bourbon nobility.

Talleyrand was a Freemason, a member of Nine Sisters Lodge in Paris, the same lodge as many of Napoleon's Generals, including Marshal Ney. Talleyrand and Wellington had met on many occasions and were cordial friends. Talleyrand had much to do before heading to Vienna. Growing concern for Napoleon's officers and their families prompted a secret mission while he visited England to secure cordial relations between the two former enemies. Talleyrand did all he could to secure cooperation in the escape and subsequent safe passage for French officers to Quebec, Britain's French - speaking province in North America.

He was unsuccessful as George IV refused any official participation in such a plan. Another way would have to be found to save Marshal Ney and the others.

Within a few days of returning to France from Britain, Talleyrand boarded a ship for America. While in Philadelphia he visited the grave of Benjamin Franklin to pay his respects. The time had finally come for repayment of a debt involving Franklin's fellow Masons of St. John's Lodge in Philadelphia.

During Franklin's nine year stay in France, as the first U.S. ambassador to France, and became very popular with the French people. He was active in Nine Sisters Lodge, where arrangements had been worked out in private for military assistance during the War of Independence. The Masonic kindness experienced by Franklin many years before would now be reciprocated in Philadelphia.

And so, with the assistance of St. John's Lodge members, numerous French military officers would be helped to enter the United States at Baltimore and Philadelphia. Then they would disappear into the countryside, most likely in the French - speaking areas of South Carolina and Louisiana.

Napoleon's Traitor. Toby Giese, New York 1989.
Ibid. p. 10
Ibid. p. 13
Ibid. p. 14
Napoleon's Marshal - The Life of Marshal Ney. John Foster, New York 1968.
Marshal Ney, A Dual Life. Legette Blythe, New York 1937
Ibid. p. 204-206
Ibid. p. 213

Marshal Ney, Before and After Execution. D. J. Edward Smoot, Charlotte 1929

So, what is the significance of Peter Ney being Marshal Ney and travelling to live in this particular area of North Carolina? Taken by itself there would be no real significance. It would simply be a coincidental occurrence. However, there are several things that appear to be more than just a coincidence.

It has been suggested that Marshal Ney wanted to live anonymously for the rest of his life and chose this rural area in order to not attract undue attention. And, if attention had been drawn to him, the remoteness of the area would significantly hinder word of his presence from leaking out. But, why this particular area? Were there not equally remote places in the new United States that would have served him just as well? Of course there were.

Ney moved to this area to keep an eye on Daniel Paseur, to be available to assist or to summon aid if needed. Regardless of which side Ney had served in France, he was still a Frenchman and was loyal to his homeland.

Before his secret exile he had owned a small farm in the Lorraine area of France, which was now under Prussian (German) rule. As you remember the French Lorraine area bordered the German Palatine. Both Provinces had large German and French speaking populations due to immigration back and forth. Another coincidence?

So what evidence do we have that Peter Stuart Ney was actually Marshal Michel Ney, General to Napoleon. Actually we do have some evidence, though it is mostly circumstantial.

From many accounts, Peter Ney's body had many scars that seemed to be from bullets and shrapnel. Once a fencing master visited the school that Ney taught at in Rowan County, NC. The students convinced Ney to spar with this master. Ney was quite a bit older than the travelling fencing master, yet he disarmed him in very short order. The fencing master left the area, telling the students that they already had a fencing master.

Ney had confessed to Rev. Basil Jones of South Carolina, that he was in fact Marshal Ney. He said that at the firing squad it was arranged for him to fake his death. He had placed a bladder of blood under his coat. The guns were loaded with blanks. When he fell, he burst the bladder and let the blood flow out upon the ground.

Ney enjoyed arriving at the school where he taught early in the morning and read the newspaper. As he was reading one morning in 1821, he saw the article, which told of Napoleon's death. Ney seemed to be obviously upset. He cancelled the classes for that day and returned to the boarding house where he lived. Later that day, he tried to commit suicide by slitting his own throat. He would have died had not other residents of the boarding house not found him. He eventually recovered.

The Reverend James A. Weston, Rector of the Protestant Episcopal Church of the Ascension in Hickory, NC published a book in the early 1900s entitled, ***Historic Doubts as to the Execution of Marshal Ney***[xix].

In that book, Reverend Weston recounted a conversation that he had with Marshal Michel Ney's son. The son stated that the day after Marshal Ney's "execution" he visited with his wife and children at their house in France. The son went on to say that when he arrived in America in 1837, he called on Peter Ney in North Carolina.

Peter Ney gave the son $1000, which he used to pay for his medical education at the Jefferson Medical College in Philadelphia. This son became a doctor and resided in Kentucky and practiced medicine there. He was interviewed when he was 88 years old and confirmed much of what had been written that Marshal Ney had escaped to America.[xx]

Peter Ney told a friend, John Rogers that he had always hoped to return to France, but those hopes had vanished now that Napoleon had died.

Marshal Ney was a Freemason of very high rank, a Rosicrucian, and a member of the Knights of the Temple (Templar?). Peter Ney always seemed live in areas where there was an active Freemason community. Many believe that one or more of these organizations aided in his escape from the firing squad and his escape to America.[xxi]

There are two significant quotes attributed to Peter Ney. He reportedly said as he was dying, "Bessieres is dead, and the Old Guard is defeated; now let me die." The second, again on his death bed his doctor asked point blank if he was Marshal Ney. Ney replied, "By all that is holy, I am Marshal Ney of France!"

Peter Stuart Ney died in Rowan County, North Carolina and is buried at the Third Creek Presbyterian Church near Cleveland, NC. The inscription on his tombstone reads: : "In memory of Peter Stuart Ney, a native of France and soldier of the French Revolution under Napoleon Bonaparte, who departed this life November 15, 1846, aged 77 years."

Chapter 5

Jean Lafitte

The story of Jean Lafitte in Lincolnton is an intriguing one. In the 1820s a man arrived in Lincolnton with a French accent and proceeded to buy up large tracts of property. He bought entire blocks in Lincolnton along with land outside the city itself. One tract in particular was in the Long Shoals area. He identified himself as Lorenzo Ferrer. It seems that he paid for everything with gold coins, many of which were minted in foreign countries.

There were many people who thought that he may have been a pirate, and some who thought that he was the pirate, Jean Lafitte.

There is a story that Ferrer once encountered Peter Ney on the streets in Lincolnton. They conversed for a few minutes in French and both became very angry. They very nearly came to blows, or perhaps were ready to duel right on the street. Acquaintances of both men separated them, and both went on about their business. So far as is known, that is the only encounter between the two men and Peter S. Ney soon afterward moved to Rowan County.

Speculation is that both French speaking people were in Lincoln County for the same reason. That reason was to assist and to keep an eye on Daniel Payseur, the Lost Dauphin. Their conversation apparently led to some disagreement as to who was in charge of that large task. Or, maybe it was how the task was to be carried out. We may never know the full story. We do know that it is rally a major coincidence that 2 men of considerable means, both French speaking, both undoubtedly having military experience and able to take care of themselves, should arrive in Lincoln County just a few years after George and Daniel Payseur arrived..

Perhaps one or both of these men were charged with returning Louis XVII (Daniel Payseur) to France.. Their motives are lot to history, but it seems unlikely. Both Frenchmen and Daniel Payseur lived to ripe old ages and there is no further evidence of any additional conflict among them.

On January 28, 2001, Lincoln County historian, Darrell Harkey was interviewed by the Hickory Daily Record Newspaper in Hickory, NC. Here's what he had to say about Lorenzo Ferrer excerpted from the newspaper.

A brick wall between white people and those who were thought to have even one drop of African blood in them divides the cemetery. Because of the racial division, Louisa Ferrer and her white husband Lorendzo are not buried side by side.

Lorendzo was thought to be a pirate and came to Lincolnton mysteriously one day and started buying entire streets &buildings in the 1820s.

"He spoke the language of sailors. He had in his possession more gold and silver than one could have accumulated in 20 lifetimes. He had in his possession the loot that gave the impression of ill-gotten gains," said Harkey.

"In the 1820s, this mysterious man shows up in Lincolnton and buys Whole blocks where my office is (West Water Street). "Lorendzo apparently bought property where the downtown apartments are on

South Aspen Street and large farms near the Hickory Grove Community and the Long Shoals Community.

Then he bought a slave for $1,000, a large amount when the average man made 50 cents a day. Despite suspicions about the origins of Lorendzo's money, Harkey said, "He was good to people. People around town liked him." Harkey said he left town and came back with a woman named Louisa, who was part black. Lorendzo wanted to marry this woman but law forbade it during the time. Lorendzo offered the Episcopal church a large sum of money, but he was declined. Rising above the social strains of the age, the interracial couple had a son together.

Everybody fussed over their son, according to Harkey, since he was an adorable child. Instead of Feeling proud, it angered Lorendzo and once he took his son's Face and put it directly in the pit of a fire. The child survived but was forever scarred. "Slaves were your property and children were too," explained Harkey.

Louisa was popular in town and was a talented, educated and beautiful woman, said Harkey. "People in town loved her, but she still wasn't white," said Harkey.
She died at the age of 40 and has an elaborate tombstone dedicated to her. Lorendzo has an even more elaborate tombstone, a larger tabletop monument with six legs.

Alfred Nixon wrote a small book or pamphlet in 1910 entitled, **<u>The History of Lincoln County</u>**. In this book, he had this to say about Lorenzo Ferrer.
An old Frenchman in Lincolnton, Lorenzo Ferrer, often bought farm products from Mr. Coon, and so admired his perfect integrity, and "full measure of potatoes," that one of his bequests was: "I will and bestow to honest George Koon one hundred dollars."

Lorenzo Ferrer, having been introduced, shall have place in this history. he was a native of Lyons, France, but spent his long life from early manhood in Lincolnton. He died August 6th, 1875, aged ninety-six years. He had his coffin made to order and gave directions concerning his grave. It is marked by a recumbent slab, supported on marble columns. The first paragraph of his will in these words:

"I, Lorenzo Ferrer, here write my last will and testament whilst I am in Possession of my faculties, as I have shortly to appear at the tribunal of St. Peter at the gate of eternity; when St. Peter is to pronounce according to my merits or demerits; for our Lord Jesus Christ entrusted the key to Heaven to St. Peter and enjoined him to admit the deserving to enter into Heaven and enjoy an eternal happiness, but to condemn the underserving defrauders to the everlasting sulphurious flames in the Devil's abode. Therefore, I am endeavoring to comfort myself in such a manner in order to merit an eternal happiness in the presence of God, and his angels, and in company with St. Peter, St. Titus and the other saints. For I am anxious to converse with those martyred saints and rejoice with them at the firmness, patience, and willingness they endured at their martyrdom for the sake of our Lord Jesus Christ. I am also in hope to see and embrace my kind an honest friends Michael Hoke, William Lander, and other good and honest friends with whom I hope to enjoy an eternal felicity,"etc.[xxii]

The life of Jean Laffite is a mystery. No one knows for certain where he was born. At various times he said that he was born in what is now Haiti, Bordeaux, France and other places.. There are several things, however, that are certain. According to Laffite himself, he was not a pirate, he was a privateer. It was said that if you called him a pirate you were likely going to have a fight on your hands.

He did aid Andrew Jackson (another Carolina native) in the Battle of New Orleans against the British during the War of 1812. Operating out of Barataria Island in the Gulf of Mexico, he made a very good living gathering booty from British ships, and some say importing slaves after their importation was outlawed by the US government. President James Madison granted Laffite a full pardon for all crimes he had committed for his service during the War of 1812.

In 1819 he disappeared from history, or so some believe. Some say he died in Columbia, South America, some say Illinois, some say Texas and some say Louisiana. In the 1940s a diary surfaced in Texas purported to be Laffite's. It appeared to be authentic and had many firsthand references to events in Laffite's life. It seems that Lincoln County, NC can make as good a case as any that Laffite lived there.

An interesting note about Laffite is his connection to Freemasonry. It cannot be said for certain that he was a Freemason. His brother Pierre, his partner in privateering was definitely a Freemason, however. Both brothers it seems always lived in areas where there was an active Freemason Lodge.

This seems to connect the Freemasons very strongly with Lincoln County. Lafitte, and Peter Ney both had strong connections to that Society. The conjecture also is that George Pesour (Payseur) was also connected by way of his membership in the Nine Sisters Lodge in Paris.

Jean Laffite

The Pirate

The connection cannot be drawn conclusively. However, it is a curious set of circumstances that several people with "French connections" were living in Lincoln County at the same time that the purported exiled King of France, Louis VII was also. Since Lincoln County was primarily comprised of descendant of German and Scots Irish immigrants, it is at least curious that several prominent Frenchmen may have called Lincoln County home.

It is also very interesting that all of these people were connected in some way with the Freemasons.

It would seem that such a strong set of coincidences would stretch the imagination at least as much as this story of Daniel Payseur does.

Chapter 6

Marquis de Lafayette

Just about every school kid knows the name Lafayette. He was one of the many heroes of the revolutionary War, and probably the most famous participant who was not American. He was born in the south central province of Auvergne in 1757 and was less than 21 years old when he came to America to serve under George Washington. His full name and title was Marie-Joseph Paul Yves Roch Gilbert du Motier, Marquis de La Fayette.

His lineage in Auvergne goes back for quite some time. His father, Gilbert de Lafayette led an army with Joan of Arc in the battle Of Orleans. It was said that another of his ancestors acquired the Crown of Thorns during the 6th Crusade in Jerusalem.

When he was 16, he married Marie Adrienne Francoise de Noailles. She was a daughter of a Duke in France and a distant relative of King George III of England.

During the Revolutionary War, Lafayette began as an aide de camp to General Washington on the recommendation of Benjamin Franklin. Franklin was then serving as ambassador to France and had met Lafayette there. Franklin had written letters of introduction for Lafayette before he left for America.

On an interesting note, both Franklin and Lafayette were Freemasons. While in Paris, Franklin was active in the Lodge of the Nine Sisters, and it could easily have been that he met Lafayette through his Masonic ties.[xxiii] Washington later made Lafayette a general in the Continental Army and he fought in many battles. Most notably were the Battle of Brandywine, where he was

wounded, at the Battle of Rhode Island. During the war he returned to France and successfully negotiated French support for the

Revolutionary cause. When he returned to America, he participated in the Battle of Yorktown, where Cornwallis finally surrendered to General Washington, effectively ending the war. One of Washington's other Generals, Benjamin Lincoln, was selected to be the one who accepted Lord Cornwallis' sword during the surrender ceremony. When Lincoln County, NC was established in 1789, it was named for General Benjamin Lincoln.

After the war, Lafayette returned to France and became active in the French political scene. He served as Vice Chairman of the Estates Generale and submitted a draft of the ***Declaration of Rights of the Common Man and of the Citizen.***

*"On 20 June 1791, an unsuccessful plot, called the **Flight to Varennes**, nearly allowed the king to escape from France. As leader of the National Guard, Lafayette had been responsible for the royal family's custody. He was thus blamed by **Danton** for the mishap and called a "traitor" to the people by **Maximilien Robespierre**. These accusations portrayed Lafayette as a royalist, and damaged his reputation in the eyes of the public.[93] The episode garnered support throughout the country for the Republican movement, and "polarized" the king's supporters."*

*"Through the latter half of 1791, Lafayette's stature continued to decline. On 17 July, the **Cordeliers** organized an event, at the Champs de Mars, to gather signatures on a petition which called for a referendum on Louis XVI -The assembled crowd, estimated to be up to 10,000, hanged two men believed to be spies after they were found under a platform."*

His participation for the monarchy, opposing the French Revolution put him in hot water with the Jacobins. He tried to flee to the United States through Holland, but was captured by the Austrians and spent 5 years in prison there.

Napoleon finally secured his release from prison. Though he refused to become a member of Napoleon's government, after the monarchy was restored, he was a member of the Chamber of Deputies in 1815 and served there until his death.

Marquis de Lafayette

In 1824, President James Monroe invited Lafayette to visit the United States as a guest of the government. This was in part to help the nation celebrate its 50th anniversary. While in the United States, Lafayette toured all 24 states covering almost 6000 miles.

*"Lafayette arrived from France at **Staten Island** in **New York**, on 15 August 1824, to an artillery salute. The towns and cities he visited, including **Fayetteville, North Carolina**, the first city named in his honour, gave him enthusiastic welcomes. During this tour he recognized and embraced James Armistead Lafayette, a **free negro** who took his last name to honor him, while in Yorktown, the story of the event was reported by the Richmond Enquirer. On 17 October 1824, Lafayette visited Mount Vernon and George Washington's tomb. On 4 November 1824, he visited Jefferson at **Monticello**, and on the 8th he attended a public banquet at the **University of Virginia** Subsequently, he accepted an invitation for honorary membership to the University's **Jefferson Literary and Debating Society**.*

*In late August 1825, he returned to Mount Vernon. A military unit decided to adopt the title National Guard, in honour of Lafayette's celebrated Garde Nationale de Paris. This battalion, later the **7th Regiment**, was prominent in the line of march when Lafayette passed through New York before returning to France on the frigate **USS Brandywine**. Late in the trip, he again received honorary citizenship of Maryland. Lafayette was feted at the first commencement ceremony of George Washington University in 1824. He was voted, by the **U.S. Congress**, the sum of $200,000 and a **township** of land located in **Tallahassee, Florida** to be known as the **Lafayette Land Grant**"*

Lafayette's secretary, Monsieur Lavasseur, kept a diary of their journeys through the United States. Here's some of that he had to say.

"On the 4th of March, we reached the pleasant little town of Fayetteville, situated on the western shore of Cape Fear river. The weather was excessively bad; the rain fell in torrents, yet the road for several miles before we reached the place was crowded with men and boys on horseback, and militia on foot; the streets of the town were filled with a throng of ladies, in full dress, hastening across the little streams of water, to approach the General's carriage, and so much occupied with the pleasure of seeing him that they appeared almost insensible of the deluge which threatened almost to swallow them up. This enthusiasm may be more readily imagined, when it is recollected that it was expressed by the inhabitants of a town founded, about forty years ago, to perpetuate the remembrance of the services rendered by him whom they honored on that day."

Upon leaving on his way to South Carolina, he offered a toast to the town. *"Fayetteville. – May it receive all the encouragements and attain all the prosperity which are anticipated by the fond and grateful wishes of its affectionate and respectful namesake."*

After visiting several towns in North Carolina, Lafayette journeyed to South Carolina, visiting the Camden Battleground and also Columbia, among other towns before moving on to Georgia.

In all his travels it seems that he made a point to visit as many Masonic Temples as possible, visiting 24 in all. In Tennessee this bit of history was uncovered.

"Earl B. Dellzell, in the "Grand Lodge Bulletin," Iowa, November, 1930, states" "In the proceedings of the Grand Lodge of Tennessee of 1825, pages 133 and 135, the minutes of the Grand Lodge of Wednesday, May 4, 1825,

state: "Our illustrious brother General Lafayette was unanimously elected an honorary member of this Grand

Lodge.' Later we find: 'Our illustrious brother General Lafayette was introduced by Bros. Andrew Jackson and G.W. Campbell, received with Grand Honors, and seated on the right of the W.W. Grand Master.' "'At the conclusion of the Grand Master's address of welcome, Lafayette made a feeling and appropriate reply, in substance as follows:' "'He felt himself highly gratified at being so kindly welcomed by the Grand Lodge of Tennessee, and at being made an honorary member of that Lodge, in which he had been introduced by the distinguished brother Mason who had erected the lines of New Orleans, and, in technical language of the Craft, had made them "well-formed, true and trusty." He had, he said, been long a member of the Order, having been initiated, young as he was, even before he entered the service of our country in the Revolutionary War. [xxiv]

Lafayette loved the United States and particularly George Washington on his tour or America, he stopped at Mt. Vernon to pay his respects at Washington's tomb. It is said that when he died in France, soil from Washington's tomb was placed on his grave.

So, where does Lafayette fit in with Daniel Payseur? The connections are circumstantial. The obvious connection would be their French connection, if in fact, Daniel Payseur was the Lost Dauphin. Since both would have been French royalty, there would have been at least some sympathetic leanings by Lafayette toward the former Crown Prince.

Lafayette was a royalist as was evidenced by his refusal to join Napoleon's government.

Lafayette was in the French military, at one time commanding the Garde Nationale. This would have given him the opportunity to have met Marshal Michel Ney. They could have perhaps been members of the same Masonic Lodge, since the evidence shows that both were very likely active Freemasons.

Lafayette was introduced at the Masonic Lodge in Tennessee by none other than Andrew Jackson. As you recall, Jackson was the commander who defeated the British at the Battle of New Orleans with the Help of Privateer Jean Laffite. Lafitte himself was French and purportedly lived in Lincolnton, NC.

These connections would seem to make it at least plausible that during Lafayette's tour of the United States, that he met with Daniel Payseur. Whether that meeting took place in Lincoln County, or more likely at a spot nearer to one of the towns he visited, cannot be proven.

Perhaps a "side trip" by both men would have been possible somewhere between Lincolnton and either Columbia or Camden. One town that comes to mind would be Lancaster, SC. Lancaster is about halfway between Lincolnton and either Columbia or Camden. Also, Lancaster does hold some significance, as we'll see later on, in the story of the Daniel Payseur family.

Chapter 7

Daniel Payseur

According to Thomas Marino in his book, Pasour, Paysour, Payseur, Paseur, Together at Last, George Pasour, Jr. was born in 1764 in Maryland. He moved to North Carolina with his father, George, Sr.,, mother, Charlotta Hetzer, and siblings,. in 1770. [xxv]

George Jr. married Hannah Hoyl in Lincoln County, NC in 1780. George and Hannah are both buried in the old Kastner Cemetery in what is now Gaston County. According to Marino, George Jr. died in 1851 and Hannah in 1844. Before their deaths they brought into the world 8 children, one of which was Daniel Payseur.

Daniel Payseur was born in 1793 and was the third son and the 4th child of George Payseur, Jr. In 1814, Daniel married Susannah Kiser in Lincoln County, NC Both Daniel and Susannah are buried in the Daniel Pasour Cemetery (now called Walnut Grove) in Gaston County, NC. Daniel passed in 1867 and Susannah in 1875. According to records they had 10 children.

This is as close as we can get to an "official" record of Daniel Payseur. [xxvi]

In a previous chapter, it was pointed out that the Dauphin, Louis Charles of France, son of Louis XVI and Marie Antoinette, was actually Daniel Payseur. There seems to be some discrepancy here. Daniel Payseur was born in 1793 and the Dauphin was born in 1785. That's a difference of 8 years. So how can that be resolved?

Maybe it can't be resolved, but here are a few considerations. Louis Charles, the Dauphin was known to be small for his age, especially after suffering a prolonged illness while imprisoned. This could account for mistaking him for a younger boy. Let's say a 2 or 3 year difference. At age 50 or so a five year difference in appearance could be so negligible as to not matter at all.

In the United States in the late 1700s and early 1800s, there was very little formal record keeping. Most birth and death records were simply a notation in a family Bible. Of course, these notations are often very accurate, particularly if the family notes them right away. However, as years go by sometimes memories become fuzzy. So the accuracy of these records is largely dependent on who made the notations and how long from the event they were made.

Daniel Payseur was the third born son of George. Yet, by all accounts in family lore there was something different about him. All of George Payseur's children lived in the same general area, from Kings Mountain, NC on up to the Lincoln County and Catawba County areas. All of them were farmers and/or dealt in trading with their friends and neighbors. All had basically the same schooling and education levels. But there were some differences.

Many family members have commented, after reading old letters written by Daniel, that he seemed to be much more educated than his brothers and sisters. His syntax, vocabulary, and even his penmanship appears to be much better than his siblings. One of his descendants once said that Daniel couldn't be a Payseur because, "he was too smart."

Also, through the years there have been persistent rumors of a chest of gold that was owned by Daniel. There have been none of these rumors associated with any of his brothers or sisters. There are even stories of this chest being buried on land once owned by Daniel, along the base of Payseur Mountain in Gaston County, NC. Some of that land is still in the Payseur family and over the years quite a few half hearted attempts have been made to locate the chest. None have been successful.

It is also interesting to note that there have been numerous individual and commercial attempts at gold mining in that area.

Some gold has been found, but so far not enough to make it a commercially viable proposition. Since not very much gold has been found, why would have people in the 1800s and later assumed that any gold would be found there? Perhaps it is because that one of the residents of that area seemed to have "more than his share" of the rare metal.

Daniel was known to have been relatively well off financially. His son, Jonas, even more well off. Where did this wealth come from? We can only surmise, but if Daniel was indeed the Lost Dauphin of France, it stands to reason that he would have had access to at least a certain amount of funds.

As you remember form an earlier chapter, Louis Charles came into an inheritance from General Kleber of over $1 million. Also with the conspiracy to hide the Dauphin and to get him out of danger, it is reasonable to assume that some of the royal possessions were able to leave the country with him. After all, his father, Louis XVI was one of, if not the richest person in all of Europe. So, even a small amount of this wealth could have been a very substantial amount.

As was also mentioned earlier, if true, the Dauphin had considerable help from King George III of England. Besides being a distant relative of the French Monarchy, King George had a fear that the revolutions in the American Colonies and in France would spread to England. As with most of the monarchs in Europe, he didn't want that to happen in his home country.

If the stories are true, it is reasonable to assume that King George III supplied young Daniel with sufficient gold and silver, along with the ship and a 600 acre land grant to assure that his time in America would not be difficult. Perhaps it was also to buy Daniel's silence to keep from implicating the English Monarchy in the Dauphin's escape.

Finally, there is a series of interesting "coincidences" that occurred during Daniel Payseur's lifetime. A Frenchman, Peter Ney came to the area. As noted earlier, Ney confessed on his deathbed that he was in fact Michel Ney, one of Napoleon's top generals and named Marshal Ney, Marshal of France. As noted in Ney's history, he served the Monarchy of France and also Napoleon, leading us to believe that he was more a French nationalist than a pure revolutionary.

A second man, Lorenzo Ferrer, arrived in Lincolnton with a French accent and an octoroon mistress. He purportedly had a chest filled with gold and silver coins, He was well known about town and owned quite a bit of real estate on Main Street in Lincolnton. It was purported that he was none other than Jean Laffite the privateer, who helped General Andrew Jackson defeat the British at the Battle of New Orleans.

Finally, in 1825 the Marquis de Lafayette visited all 24 states of the United States of America. It is well documented that Lafayette was a noted French nationalist having served in the governing bodies of both the Monarchy and the Revolutionary governments. It is also well documented that Lafayette visited Fayetteville, NC, Camden, SC, Columbia, SC, and Nashville TN. It would not be beyond the realm of possibility that those journeys brought him very close to Lincoln and Gaston Counties.

Three very prominent French military men arriving in the Lincoln County vicinity during the first quarter of the 19th century, at first glance would seem to be much more than a coincidence. Though Lincolnton was a fairly prominent frontier town at that time, it did not have the prominence of Charleston, Savannah, New York, Boston, Philadelphia, or many other cities that could be named.

Lincolnton was still an out of the way town on the edge of the frontier, not a nationally prominent o even prominent on the state.

So why did these men come to Lincolnton? Who can say for certain? Speculation has been that all three of these men arrived to "check up" on a certain resident. Maybe to offer assistance. Maybe to deliver messages either from or to France. It is likely no one will ever know. It does, however, seem to stretch credibility to assume that three of the most prominent French military leaders of the time coincidentally visited Lincolnton, NC during a 15-20 year span.

Chapter 8

Jonas Payseur

Jonas Payseur was born in Lincoln County in 1819. He was the second child born to Daniel Payseur and the first born son. Jonas married Harriett Smith in 1845. She was also born in Lincoln County, NC and her date of birth was Christmas Day in 1823. In 1884 Jonas died and was buried in Pleasant Grove Methodist Church Cemetery between the Crouse and Howards Creek areas of Lincoln County. Harriett lived until 1905 and she, too, was buried at Pleasant Grove.[xxvii]

There are many stories on the internet that state that Adam Payseur was Daniel's oldest son. Some even say that he was murdered at a young age and that the circumstances of his murder are still very much a mystery. The fact is, Adam was the younger brother of Jonas. Adam was actually born in 1833 and lived to the ripe old age of 86, dying in 1919. He was laid to rest in the Pasour Cemetery in Gaston County, and as far as anyone knows he still remains there.

The internet stories about his murder are a concoction designed to show some kind of nefarious connection to a conspiracy concerning Daniel's estate. These stories imply that the Daniel's estate was "stolen" from Adam to give to Jonas. It is simply untrue.

What is true is that often the eldest son received the bulk of the estate when the parents passed away. If that was indeed the case with Daniel, then Jonas would have been the rightful heir and there would have been no conspiracy at all.

It appears that must have been the case. Jonas was known to have had at least a moderate amount of money in contrast with his brothers and sisters. Shortly before the Civil War, Jonas began buying property. Much of this property was within the city limits of Lincolnton, close to the property that Lorenzo Ferrer was himself buying. As you may remember from an earlier chapter, Ferrer was suspected to have been noted French privateer Jean Laffite and was rumored to have had a chest filled with gold and silver coins.

It is not known whether Jonas Payseur and Lorenzo Ferrer knew each other though it can be assumed that they did. Both men were very active in the land acquisition business within the City of Lincolnton, so it would not be surprising that they would have run into each other on numerous occasions. Perhaps they even consulted with each other. Or even, to stretch a point, perhaps Ferrer was an advisor to the oldest son of the Lost Dauphin.

Jonas' acquisition of property came to a sudden end with the beginning of the Civil War. It seems that not only did he stop buying property, but actually sold quite a bit of what he had acquired. As the War dragged on, Jonas finally went bankrupt. There was some speculation about this as it came on pretty fast. Many people suspected that he was not really in as dire straits as it appeared, but rather was trying to hide his wealth from the Yankee troops that were expected to enter the area at any time. After the Civil War, Jonas took a very low profile. There was no more extensive buying or selling and Jonas settled into a life of farming. As with his father, Daniel, there have been persistent rumors over the years that Jonas also had a chest filled with gold and silver buried on his property.

This is rather curious that both Daniel and his primary heir, Jonas were believed by many to have such "treasure chests." None of their other siblings were thought to have such riches. So why is that? Nothing is really known, but there is speculation. If Daniel had been the Lost Dauphin, then he obviously had access to a certain amount of money or precious metals. Since Jonas was his heir, it would have passed down to him. As a further curiosity both Jonas and Lorenzo Ferrer, were rumored to have such chests filled with gold and silver. It has been shown that both men could have very easily known each other. It is not a tremendous leap to assume that they discussed how to manage their treasures.

Jonas Payseur

Not only is there a possibility that both men were of French extraction, but it is distinctly possible that both had strong Freemason connections. Jean Laffite's brother was definitely a Freemason and it is suspected that Jean Laffite was also, as was Ferrer suspected of being the famous privateer.

The Masonic connection, though not proven conclusively, is definitely circumstantial, as is the French Connection. Let's summarize it.

Daniel Payseur is suspected of being the Crown Prince, the Lost Dauphin of France, the son of Louis XVI and Marie Antoinette. It was stated by several family members that he seemed to be very well educated, an assertion that was never made about his brothers and sisters. He lives in the Lincoln County area of North Carolina and is suspected of having a treasure trove of gold and silver, which he passed on to his oldest son, Jonas.

At the same time that Daniel Payseur and Jonas Payseur are living in the Gaston and Lincoln County areas, a mysterious Frenchman Peter Stuart Ney moves into the vicinity. Ney is well educated and is a master swordsman. His body is covered with many scars that appear to be battle scars. He has an interest in the news of Europe and attempts suicide when hearing of the death of Napoleon. Finally, on his deathbed, Peter Stuart Ney confesses to being Michel Ney, Marshal of France and one of Napoleon's top generals.

The Marquis de Lafayette, hero of the Revolutionary War and a devoted French nationalist visited the United States at the invitation of President James Monroe in 1825. He visited every state including Fayetteville, North Carolina, Columbia, South Carolina, and Nashville, Tennessee. In those travels it is likely he could have passed close to Lincoln or Gaston Counties in NC. During his visit to Tennessee he was hosted and introduced by General Andrew Jackson at the Masonic Lodge in Nashville. Jackson, also a native North Carolinian grew up only about 50 miles from Lincoln County.

General Jackson gained national fame when he commanded the troops against the British at the Battle of New Orleans during the War of 1812. By just about every account, that battle would not have been won without the help of French Privateer, Jean Laffite.

After the War of 1812, in the first third of the 19th century another mysterious Frenchman arrived in Lincolnton. His name was Lorenzo Ferrer (his initials "LF" are the same as LaFitte as it was sometimes spelled.) He arrived with an octoroon mistress who North Carolina law would not allow him to marry. Eyewitnesses reported that he had a chest filled with gold and silver coins. In fact, in his later years, many of the young boys in town referred to him as the "old pirate." He bought much property in downtown Lincolnton at the same time that Jonas Payseur was also buying property in Lincolnton.

All of this could be a grand coincidence, but it does stretch the imagination. Is there a "French connection," a royal connection, and a Freemason connection to the history of Lincoln County?

Chapter 9

Jesse James

Jesse James and his brother, Frank were two of the most notorious outlaws in the old west. They both fought in the Civil War on the Confederate side and were members of Quantrill's Raiders. They fought as guerillas and were not a part of an organized army. Both men were accused of committing atrocities against Yankee soldiers during the war.

After the war they teamed up with the Younger boys robbing banks, trains and stagecoaches..

Jesse James was born in Missouri in 1847. After the Civil War he spent most of his time there, though he did rob banks and trains from Minnesota to Texas. He suffered two serious chest wounds that nearly killed him, but he pulled through.

After a failed bank robbery in Northfield Minnesota, Jesse returned home to Missouri. According to newspaper accounts he was murdered, shot in the back of the head by Bob Ford, a member of his gang.

Jesse and Frank James were recognized by the common people of the Midwest as a sort of Robin Hood. He often did not rob the passengers on the trains, instead confining himself to the safe. He was somewhat of a folk hero, thanks in part to his friendship with a Missouri newspaper editor. Jesse often wrote letters to the editor, which were published in the paper.

After his death there was a very popular song that further enhanced his reputation.

The Outlaw Jesse James

There are many people then and now who do not believe that Jesse James was actually killed by Bob Ford. In fact there are many people later on who claimed to be the real Jesse James. It was well known that James used many aliases during his lifetime and some of those who claimed to be the outlaw had the same name as some of his aliases.

So what does the outlaw Jesse James have to do with the Payseurs of Lincoln and Gaston County? Here's where the story gets interesting and more than a little speculative.

One alias that Jesse James used was "Claud Smith." It is believed by some that Jesse James' family was from a group that migrated from North Carolina to Kentucky and on into Missouri. Several of those family members were named Smith. As you may recall, Jonas Payseur was married to Harriet Smith. That, in and of itself, is no connection. But, there are photographs of Jesse James visiting with unnamed relatives in South Carolina in the 1870s. It seems that on several occasions, when it got too hot in Missouri, the James gang would hide out in Florida. Perhaps on his way to Florida, he stopped off to see Harriet or some of her children.[xxviii]

Greg Payseur, retired teacher, tells of one day about 20 years ago when a woman brought an antique tintype photograph to his classroom. The image on the photo was of Jesse James visiting some unknown relatives in South Carolina. She stated that the photo had been handed down in her family for many years.

But it gets even more interesting. In the early 2000s there was an auction of historical memorabilia in Florence, Kentucky. One of the items was a flint lock rifle that was given to Jesse James on his 15th birthday. It had an engraved inscription on it, which read,

"Le Dauphin," As you recall, that was the title given to the Crown Prince of France, Louis Charles. Stories claim that he came to the USA and took the name of Daniel Payseur. Daniel's son was Jonas, who married Harriet Smith. Could Harriet Smith have been one of Jesse James, aka Claud Smith's relatives?

Once again we have another coincidence concerning the French Connection.

Chapter 10
Lewis Cass Payseur

Probably no member of the Payseur family has had more written about him than Lewis Cass Payseur. If you conduct a Google search on the internet, you will find page after page on Lewis Cass. Some of it might even be true. Most of what you will find, however, are copies of articles and excerpts from Ickes' and Christopher's books. Almost all of that information is identical, if not copied word for word.

Lewis Cass Payseur (he went by the name of Cass) was born in Lincoln County, NC on October 18, 1850. He was the oldest child of Jonas Payseur and Harriet Smith Payseur. In 1874, Cass married Mary Alice Hudson in Spartanburg, SC . Later they moved to Lancaster, SC for most of their lives. Both are buried in the Westside Cemetery in Lancaster. Both of them lived long lives, with Mary Alice dying in 1934 and Cass in 1939.

They had 5 children. One died as an infant and the other 4 lived long lives.

As was mentioned in the chapter on Jonas Payseur, in the time before the Civil War, Jonas bought quite a bit of land. Much of it was within the city limits of Lincolnton, NC. In 1869, Jonas declared for bankruptcy. Many people over the years have assumed that Jonas did so to protect most of his assets from the carpetbaggers who were moving into the area.

However, only 5 years later, Jonas' son, Lewis Cass Payseur arrived in Lancaster, SC with a young wife in tow and opened a store in downtown Lancaster.

Unknown child, Pearl Mignon Payseur Poore, Lewis Cass Payseur, Harriet Smith Payseur

Cass' store was located in a building that became known as the Payseur Building. He sold jewelry, clocks, watches and other items to the general public. He owned the Payseur Building.

In buying that building and his store inventory, it seems to be pretty evident that Cass had to have had access to at least some capital. It's hardly possible to buy real estate and inventory without some cash. This tends to lend credence to the speculation that his father, Jonas, still had some substantial assets and was able to help his 24 year old son.

Cass' business began to prosper and within a few years he branched out into other areas of commerce. He was one of, if not the principal mover in the creation of the Bank of Lancaster, of which he was a major stockholder. He became a major owner of the Lancaster & Chester Railroad.

The Lancaster & Chester Railroad (L&C) was a spur line that ran between those two towns. The line delivered goods and mail to Lancaster and stopped in front of the Payseur Building. People from Lancaster and the surrounding area would travel to the Payseur Building to pick up their mail and goods that they had ordered through the mail.

Businesses in the area received shipments from the L&C. This was arranged so that these businesses did not have to pick up their goods. The railroad owned one of the first commercial "trucking' and freight hauling companies in the area. It consisted of several wagons, which loaded the freight to be delivered at the depot in front of the Payseur Building and delivered the goods to the area businesses.

One of the L&C's major freight customers was the Lancaster Manufacturing Company (LMC). The LMC was one of the first textile manufacturing companies in the area and it was owned by Cass Payseur and his partner, Leroy Springs. This company later went on to become Springs Industries. Springs Industries has long been one of the most prominent textile manufacturers in the world.

Lewis Cass Payseur, with a few other people, began the First Baptist Church of Lancaster, SC. He was instrumental in raising the money for the church building, and bought the first organ that they had. His wife, Mary Alice was the first organist of the church. She served in that capacity for many years.

Besides being very involved in the church and the business arenas of Lancaster, the Cass Payseur family was also known for their parties. There are many references in the newspaper about those "get togethers." Years ago, every newspaper had a social section which detailed some of the things that the elite in the community were involved in. many of these articles noted the parties that were hosted by Mary Alice. There were also frequent mention of the trips they had taken.

So, where did Cass's money come from to do all these things? Obviously, his businesses were very successful. But, where did the money come from to start these businesses?

If you recall in the chapters on Daniel Payseur and Jonas Payseur, there have been persistent rumors over the years of a secret treasure. In both cases the story was of a chest filled with gold and silver. There are even tales of this chest being buried on the property. The part about being buried is likely not true, as much of that property has been farmed and now developed over the years. Both the farming and development entailed at least some excavation and it is likely that the treasure would have turned up by now.

However, what if the gold and silver had been passed down from generation to generation? This seems to make more sense and will make even more as we go along.

All indications are that if there ever was such a chest, it originated with Daniel Payseur, who passed it to his oldest son, Jonas, who in turn passed it to his oldest son, Cass.

No concrete evidence has ever turned up that there ever was a chest full of gold and silver belonging to any of these people. No Concrete evidence has ever turned up that Daniel Payseur was the "Lost Dauphin." But if Daniel was, it would be the solution to many of these mysteries that have been outlined in this book.

Having said that there is no concrete evidence, it should be noted that there is some circumstantial evidence that should be, at the least discussed just a bit.

Cass Payseur was very involved in his businesses for much of his life. It was only at the very end of his life that he turned over much of the operations to his children's families. One interesting note is that during the Great Depression, the Bank of Lancaster never had and very serious problems. The assumption has always been that it was very well capitalized. It has been conjectured that most of that capital came from Cass.

One of Cass' daughters said in an interview many years ago that her dad made much of his money in the store. She stated that most of the gold used for the making of jewelry and watch cases came from gold mines that he owned. That seemed to be a curious statement since very few of the many gold mines in the NC and SC areas actually recovered very much gold. Certainly, not many of them mined enough to fill a jewelry store.

There as at least one exception to that, though. That was the Reed Gold Mine just outside of Concord NC. We have seen records that stated that Jonas Payseur was a stockholder in that mine. How large a stockholder is not certain. It would seem that the reference to gold mines could have been an attempt to conceal the actual source of the gold, perhaps it came from an inherited chest.

There is one other unsubstantiated story concerning Cass Payseur's wealth. It goes like this. Upon Cass' death, the family gathered to read the will and to inventory his assets. At the time Cass was living with his daughter in Alabama, but at his death the entire family gathered in Lancaster, SC where Lewis Cass and Mary Alice are buried.

When they opened the safe in Cass' office the family, it was told, were shocked. Though they knew all along that their father was quite wealthy, they never imagined the extent of that wealth until they looked inside the safe. No one knows exactly what they found there. Most certainly there were stock certificates form many companies that Cass had an interest in. It is likely that there was a substantial

amount of cash, and probably a large amount of gold, silver, and precious stones used in the jewelry business. There are no records of the family ever discussing the contents of the safe with anyone who wasn't there when it was opened. If they did, it was likely only with trusted counsel, who are unwilling to talk about it.

There are several people alive today in Lancaster, SC who imply that they know of some things. Those few who will admit it will not speak as they state they have been sworn to secrecy.

So what are these secrets? We can only speculate, but we can be certain that there are things that the family does not want to be made public for whatever reason. A close family member has recently decided to attempt to get to the bottom of this mystery. He has made several trips to Lancaster and has spoken to people who know much more than they will tell. He is planning more trips and more interviews.

The interesting thing about Lewis Cass Payseur is not that he amassed a certain amount of wealth during his lifetime. Many people have done that to a greater or lesser degree. The interesting point is how did he get stated in amassing this wealth? Where did the initial capital come from?

In 1902 a book was published by Garlington Publishing Company of Spartanburg, SC. It was actually more of an encyclopedia, in several volumes, of prominent men in South Carolina at the time. The author was J.C. Garlington, who more than likely owned the publishing company. Entitled, *MEN OF THE TIME. SKETCHES OF LIVING NOTABLES. A BIOGRAPHICAL ENCYCLOPEDIA OF CONTEMPORANEOUS SOUTH CAROLINA LEADERS.* Here is what it said about Lewis Cass Payseur:

PAYSEUR, L. C. Started with a few hundred dollars and has made a success. He was born in Lincolnton, North Carolina, October 18, 1850. Only a common school education. He was head clerk in J. A. Henneman's jewelry store at Spartanburg, South Carolina, four years. Married Miss Mary A. Hudson, a niece of Judge J. H. Hudson, October 18, 1874. Mayor of Lancaster for two years, and director in the Bank of Lancaster, since its organization; also director in Lancaster Cotton Mill six years.

If that had been Cass' entire biography, most people would have considered him to be quite a success. There seems to be more, however. Without there being more to the Lewis Cass Payseur story, it would be extremely difficult to explain all the tales that have cropped up all over the internet concerning, him.

There are way too many of these stories to try to debunk them all, but all of them seem to start from the same basic premise. That Lewis Cass Payseur was one of the most powerful men in America until Leroy Springs stole his wealth from him. That the Payseur family, though not the most powerful family in America anymore, is still one of the 13 most powerful families of the Illuminati. It is obviously untrue to anyone who would care to check the facts.

Here's how the story goes. LC Payseur amassed great fortune in Lancaster SC, owning textile manufacturing plants, lumber companies, and railroads. He hired a young Leroy Springs to work for him. During the Civil War many records that were stored in local court houses were transferred to the State Capitol for safe keeping. The Union Army had garnered a reputation for burning towns, particularly court houses. During this transfer, many of the records were lost.

After the war, Leroy Springs either recreated the lost records, or simply created new records showing Springs as the owner of these companies, in effect stealing them from Cass Payseur.

Let's see how this story holds up from the facts that we know. Lewis Cass Payseur was born in 1850, which would have made him 10 or 11 years old when the Civil War began and 14 or 15 when it ended. If any records were moved to the State Capitol, it is highly unlikely to nearly impossible that Lewis Cass Payseur's name was on any of them. Lewis Cass Payseur was living in Lincoln County, NC according to the 1870 census, so he couldn't have hired Leroy Springs until sometime after that since he likely had never even heard of him.

Since Cass Payseur arrived in Lancaster in 1874 and opened his jewelry store, his other business investments had to have occurred after that date. He was a partner with Leroy Springs in several business ventures including textiles and the L&C Railroad, but it seems a stretch to think that it would have been necessary for anyone to change any ownership records.

There is another item that is often cited on the internet. It is that the Bank of Lancaster of which Cass was a stock holder and director, later evolved into NationsBank and finally into Bank of America.

Without going back too far in history, NCNB was the bank that eventually became Bank of America. NCNB was chartered in North Carolina, the Bank of Lancaster was chartered in South Carolina. Through mergers and acquisitions, after the change of the interstate banking laws, NCNB began its rapid growth. This growth was largely at the direction of Hugh McCall in the 1980s and 1990s.

Until those interstate banking laws were changed, it would have been impossible for a South Carolina bank to purchase, merge, or otherwise combine with a North Carolina bank. Since those laws were not changed until the last quarter of the 20th century, Cass Payseur could have had nothing to go with interstate banking whatsoever. He had been dead for 30 years or so. Now, it would not be surprising to find that Bank of America subsequently bought the Bank of Lancaster, but not with Cass' approval or instigation.

Certainly the Bank of Lancaster could not possibly buy Bank of America. These assertions on the internet seem to be completely false.

There are many other assertions on the internet that seem to come from the same 2 sources. They state that Lewis Cass Payseur had Rockefellers, Vanderbilts, Morgans, and even Rothschilds working for him. They state that he was the principal owner of just about any major corporation in the USA. They state that he always required that he be issued stock certificate #!, which held special privileges within the company.

Whether any of that is true or not, there is one thing that is true. A detailed search will not turn up one shred of physical evidence to support those claims. Nowhere is there a copy of Stock Certificate #1 from any of the companies that are always mentioned. All anyone can find is a list that was obviously created by someone to prove a point. All will state that they were taken from public records, but no copies of those public records are ever produced. Since nothing can be produced, the only assumption once can make is that they are false.

There can be very little doubt that Lewis Cass Payseur was a wealthy man. No one denies that. There is considerable doubt and questions as to whether his wealth is or was as extensive as is often claimed.

The extent of his wealth is not the question. What is the question is how did he get started? Where did the initial "seed" money come from? Is there any truth to the "French Connection?" Did this connection enable this particular line of the Payseur family to maintain and increase their wealth?

Currently there are no answers to these and many more questions. There are only coincidences and circumstantial evidence. Perhaps further research may yet turn up the answers. This book is

an attempt to lay out these coincidences. The most interesting story is not about Lewis Cass Payseur, but rather the Daniel Payseur story.

Epilog

Doing the research for this book was quite interesting. I ran across a lot of things that I decided not to include in this book. For example, I didn't include anything about the Payseur family being shape shifting, reptilian aliens from a galaxy far, far away. I didn't include it for a simple reason. Being a Payseur, and a direct linear descendant of Daniel Payseur, I have never found myself shifting my shape, neither have I noticed any scaly outcroppings anywhere on my body. For that matter I have never noticed those things on my brothers, sisters or myriad of cousins. Believe it or not, I decided that it probably wasn't true.

I also confirmed that you can find a whole lot of "stuff" on the internet. Some of it is even true. Unfortunately quite a bit of it is not. I'll speak to that a little bit later.

Now, is everything in this book true? Probably not. But I did try to stick with the facts, and when I speculated, I believe it was pretty evident to most readers. So, as far as I can determine everything in here is factual except where I obviously speculate.

I recently finished reading a very good book by Stephen King, *11-22-63*. I am a big Stephen King fan, and I think all of his books are very good. This one is about a guy who goes back in time to try to stop the John Kennedy assassination. I won't say more about the story line than that.

There is one thing, however, that King keeps talking about in the book when he discusses that relationship between the past, the present and the future. It is something that he calls harmonics.

Harmonics is kind of a cause and effect, but it is more than that. Without getting to deep into something that I only marginally understand, and would surely say something wrong, I'll just do a very big injustice to his concept by using a brief summary.

Time is not necessarily linear. We all understand that things from the past have a direct effect on the present and future. Physicists would say that the present and the future also have a direct effect on the past. They would also say that simply by observing something, you actually have an effect on its physical characteristics. It's a quantum physics kind of thing that I really don't understand. But, it realities to the "harmony" or the "harmonics" of the universe.

Let me give you an example. As I was researching and writing this book, I contacted several of my relatives to get some genealogical information. Some couldn't tell me any more than I had already found out, but they could and did confirm some of my research.

I was just getting ready to begin my chapter on Daniel Payseur, aka the Lost Dauphin, and emailed my cousin, Greg Payseur, for some information. After going back and forth through several emails, he suggested that he could talk much faster than he could type, so he called me.

We talked about a lot of things that had some relevance to this book. He told me many things I wasn't aware of and I told him a few things that he wasn't aware of, such as the existence of some handwritten letters of Daniel's.

One of the more interesting things he mentioned was that there was a distant relative of ours who had in his possession the original tombstones of Daniel, his wife Susannah, and 6 other of his family members. Due to some kind of change at the cemetery they had been buried in, he had to remove the head stones. They didn't fit in with what the cemetery wanted to do there.

He has kept these headstones stored in his barn for over 25 years. Now, due to health issues, he was planning to tear down the barn and would no longer be able to store them. He wanted to keep them in the "family." He asked Greg if he could help out.

As I write this, Greg and I are planning to go retrieve these monuments for safe keeping. By the time this book is published, we hope to have a permanent home for them in a different historic cemetery, near where the family originally lived.
There is another thing that I learned from Greg. He told me that you can learn quite a bit just from looking at tombstones. Greg has tried to find the graves of many of our ancestors and has visited the cemeteries as much as possible.. Here is the interesting fact about the Daniel payseur family. Daniel Payseur, Jonas Payseur, and Lewis Cass Payseur, all have the largest and most impressive head stones, for their time, in the cemeteries in which they are buried. That implies a certain amount of wealth. Another coincidence?

Harmonics.

The obvious question is, "why not remove the bodies and rebury them in the different cemetery?" That is very valid. It appears after doing a little bit of literal digging at the original cemetery, there were no graves underneath these headstones. Over 150 years these stones were reset, realigned and eventually came to rest over a spot where there were no graves. Daniel and his family are still buried there, only not where the headstones were set. So, one place is as good as another.

Again, harmonics.

My reasons for writing this book were twofold. First, I thought it was an interesting story. The possibility that the "Lost

Dauphin" escaped to American, and might be related to me was actually kind of cool. That was got me started.

What kept me going were the seemingly implausible coincidences that kept coming up. All of the French people who began appearing in and around Lincoln County, NC; Daniel had a chest full of gold and silver; Jonas had a chest full of gold and

silver; Lewis Cass had a chest full of gold and silver; Lorenzo Ferrer had a chest full of gold and silver; Jonas went bankrupt in 1869, yet 10 years later his son, Lewis Cass was one of the most prominent businessmen in Lancaster, SC; that the Payseur family, an obscure family from an obscure part of North Carolina could be cited all

over the internet as one of the most powerful families in the world, especially when my personal experiences old me otherwise: all of this kept me looking. And, it helped me to find even more coincidences and things that just didn't add up.

Now let me talk about the internet. It seems that most of the references to the Payseur family on the internet as being "in charge" of basically, the world, can be traced back to one of 2 sources: a man named David Ickes, and another person named Alex Christopher (not sure is Alex is a man or a woman. I've seen it referenced both ways.). Just about everyone who cites tales about the Payseurs, if they are not citing each other, cite one of these people.

Much of the information is just plain wrong. Some of that has been pointed out earlier in this book. There are other things, minor things, that tend to make the reader wonder about the quality of research that these people have done, or if they have done any research at all.

Dozens of websites refer to one of Lewis Cass Payseur's daughters as LALA or IALA, I'm using capital letters so there is no mistaking the spelling. Her name is IOLA. They refer to Jonas

Payseur's wife as HARRIETTA. Her name is HARRIETT. If they can't get the names right, how much more is wrong.

When you search the internet for anything referring to Lewis Cass or Jonas Payseur, you will often see these exact sentences in dozens of so-called "original" websites.

"Now most Americans have to ask, who is LC Payseur?", or
"Jonas married Harrietta Smith and they had Lewis Cass Payseur"

Not very original and also not very correct. It is remarkable that so many "original websites use the exact same sentences with the exact same errors. They are all copying from each other. There is no research being done at all or else some of these people would correct those mistakes.

Admittedly, in the greater scheme of things, these are very minor errors. But how can you trust someone to have the facts correct when they can't even take the time to check the spelling of a few words.

I emailed David Ickes a couple of times to ask where he got his information from, and of course, got no reply. If you conduct a Google search, you'll see the same text come up over and over again. Often they are not even cited, but they all read the same, usually word for word.

Finally when you search the web, you will find all kinds of information about the Payseur family being one of the 13 most powerful families of the Illuminati. That's pretty interesting, until you find that we are also Satanist reptiles from outer space. Well, maybe we are, but if so, I'm missing out on a whole lot of stuff.

So, there you have it. I hope that you found this book interesting. I also hope that it will spur you into further research. I am convinced that there are members of the Payseur family who have old letters or documents that could either prove or disprove many of the tings mentioned in this book. Let's hope they turn up.

References

[i] Marino, Thomas J., ***Pasour, Paysour Payseur, Paseur, Together At Last***, Birmingham Publishing Company, 1992

[ii] Schulze, Lorine McGinnis,OliveTreeGenealogyhttp://olivetreegenealogy.com/ Copyright © 1996

[iii] ibid. Marino, Thomas, ***Pasour, Paysour ...***

[iv] ibid. Marino, Thomas J, ***Pasour, Paysour…***

[v] http://i2.photobucket.com/albums/y38/Bjordi/5-29-20116-22-08PM.jpg

[vi] Ibid, http://i2.photobucket.com/albums/y38/Bjordi/5-29-20116-22-08PM.jpg

[vii] Ibid, http://i2.photobucket.com/albums/y38/Bjordi/5-29-20116-22-08PM.jpg

[viii] Ibid., http://i2.photobucket.com/albums/y38/Bjordi/5-29-20116-24-35PM.jpg

[ix] http://www.napoleonguide.com/kleber.htm

[x] Ibid., http://www.napoleonguide.com/kleber.htm

[xi] Ibid., http://www.napoleonguide.com/kleber.htm

[xii] Ibid., http://www.napoleonguide.com/kleber.htm

[xiii] Ibid., http://www.napoleonguide.com/kleber.htm

[xiv] Ibid., Marino, ***Thomas, Pasour, Paysour…***

[xv] Historic Doubts as to the Execution of Marshal Ney by James A. Weston (N.Y.: Whittaker, 1895)

[xvi] Napoleon's Traitor. Toby Giese, New York 1989
[xvii] Napoleon's Marshal - The Life of Marshal Ney. John Foster, New York 1968
[xviii] *Marshal Ney, A Dual Life.* Legette Blythe, New York 1937

[xix] Weston, James A, ***Historic Doubts as to the Execution of Marshal Ney.***

[xx] *http://blackmerlodge.org/wp-content/uploads/2010/12/PETER-STUART-NEY.pdf*
[xxi] Weston, James A, ***Historic Doubts as to the Execution of Marshal Ney.***
[xxii] Nixon, Alfred, **The History of Lincoln County**, 1910
[xxiii] *Short Talk Bulletin,* vol. vi, no.7 (July 1928); vol. xi, no. 7 (July 1933); vol xii, no. 4 (April 1934). *The New Age* magazine, July 1941. Illustration: "Gilbert Mottier Lafayette,
[xxiv] Earl B. Dellzell, in the "Grand Lodge Bulletin," Iowa, November, 1930
[xxv] Ibid., Marino, Thomas, ***Thomas, Pasour, Paysour…***
[xxvi] Ibid., Marino, Thomas, ***Thomas, Pasour, Paysour…***
[xxvii] Ibid., Marino, Thomas, ***Thomas, Pasour, Paysour…***
[xxviii] **http://genforum.genealogy.com/outlaws/messages/3476.html**

www.ingramcontent.com/pod-product-compliance
Lightning Source LLC
Chambersburg PA
CBHW032018040426
42448CB00006B/655